Standing in the
PRESENCE OF
GREATNESS

"Thousands of young people have been blessed by David Kohout and his message that Talk is Cheap. The real story of how this passion to serve others has exploded is spectacular. Through his presentations, and now his book, David will continue to be a difference-maker to countless young people in much the same fashion that I have personally witnessed him do so with our students at Youngstown State and Ohio State. Thank you for serving others, David!"

—**Jim Tressel**, President, Youngstown State University and former coach, Youngstown State University Penguins and Ohio State Buckeyes. Author; *The Winners Manual, Life Promises for Success: Promises from God on Achieving Your Best*

"As a person who has built a business assisting others in achieving their financial dreams, I believe this book truly does motivate, encourage, and remind us that average is the best of the worst and the worst of the best, as well as that if you want to achieve GREATNESS, you can't settle for anything but doing the best you can, accepting nothing less."

—**Bob Sebo**, Retired Senior Vice President, PAYCHEX

"There are times when you come across people who make an impact on your life in some way that changes you either for better or worse. Usually in those times you know right away that the person is for real and that they truly are trying to make a difference. To me, success is measured by how much you are able to help people, not by how much you make or what level education you have or what social status you have attained. This leads me to Dave Kohout.

I met David somewhere around 2006 when I was the superintendent at Columbiana Exempted Village Schools. I was approached by my middle school principal about an opportunity to have a motivational speaker come to meet and talk with the students. I was given Dave's name and immediately made a few phone calls to do some background, which unfortunately in this day and age is a necessity. Of course Dave was given great recommendations from the area administrators who had heard him and allowed him to speak to kids.

I have been a football coach and have been involved with the Fellowship of Christian Athletes since I was a sophomore in high school so I had some experience with allowing speakers to talk motivationally to student athletes. I wasn't exactly sure how it would work in front of an entire group of public school students, nor how it would be perceived among staff and parents, but I took a shot and invited Dave in to speak.

Needless to say it didn't take me long to realize the sincerity and compassion in his words. The impact on the students was profound. I made a conscious decision that day to try and help David reach more students in any way possible. I was fortunate to become the Superintendent for the Mahoning County Educational Service Center. My position has allowed me to recommend Dave to many school districts for motivational speeches to students and to help in professional development for teachers and administrators.

I am fortunate to have known Dave for the time I have and will continue to help him change lives for as long as I am able. David is without a doubt one of those people that I have met that impacts lives in a very positive way, including my own.

—**Ron Iarussi**, Superintendent,
Mahoning County Educational Service Center

"I have to honestly say that the 60 minutes he shared had an enormous impact on both the students and the adults. His balance of positive energy, humor, and emotion sends his message 'bone deep'. Our school is a different place since Dave spoke to us."

—**Tim Saxton**, Superintendent, Boardman Local Schools

"I have been in education and administration for 41 years and can honestly say nobody I have come across has even come close to making a difference in a school as David has done. What an amazing impact he had on the students, staff, and entire community."

—**John Young**, former Principal,
Cardinal Mooney High School

Standing in the
PRESENCE OF
GREATNESS

DISCOVER SEVEN REAL LIFE ACCOUNTS OF GREATNESS ALONG MY JOURNEY THUS FAR

David Kohout & Kathleen Palumbo

NEW YORK

NASHVILLE   MELBOURNE

Standing in the PRESENCE OF **GREATNESS**
DISCOVER SEVEN REAL LIFE ACCOUNTS OF GREATNESS ALONG MY JOURNEY THUS FAR

© 2017 David Kohout & Kathleen Palumbo

Published in New York, New York, by Morgan James Publishing. Morgan James and The Entrepreneurial Publisher are trademarks of Morgan James, LLC.
www.MorganJamesPublishing.com

The Morgan James Speakers Group can bring authors to your live event. For more information or to book an event visit The Morgan James Speakers Group at www.TheMorganJamesSpeakersGroup.com.

Shelfie

A **free** eBook edition is available
with the purchase of this print book.

CLEARLY PRINT YOUR NAME ABOVE IN UPPER CASE

Instructions to claim your free eBook edition:
1. Download the Shelfie app for Android or iOS
2. Write your name in **UPPER CASE** above
3. Use the Shelfie app to submit a photo
4. Download your eBook to any device

ISBN 978-1-68350-080-3 paperback
ISBN 978-1-68350-081-0 eBook
Library of Congress Control Number:
2016907708

Cover Design by:
Megan Whitney
megan@creativeninjadesigns.com

Interior Design by:
Bonnie Bushman
The Whole Caboodle Graphic Design

Morgan James Builds

The Entrepreneurial Publisher™

with...

Habitat for Humanity®
Peninsula and
Greater Williamsburg

In an effort to support local communities, raise awareness and funds, Morgan James Publishing donates a percentage of all book sales for the life of each book to Habitat for Humanity Peninsula and Greater Williamsburg.

Get involved today! Visit
www.MorganJamesBuilds.com

To the six most important people in my life:

Mom and dad — I wouldn't be here without you!

To Jesus Christ; All praise and honor to You!
There is no other name; because of You, I've been
born twice and will die only once. Wow!

To my high school sweetheart and bride
since 11am on May 4th, 1985. I love you!

My babies, David Michael (26), and Courtney Lynn (28);
you will always be my favorite son and daughter! ☺

Contents

FOREWORD

Concerning the ULTIMATE GREATNESS and the other greatness.

During his presentations before tens of thousands of students in hundreds of venues across our land and abroad, my eternal friend and dear brother in Christ, David Kohout, never fails to tell them, "You are standing in the presence of greatness." In my estimation, that is a double entendre.

On the one hand, they are in the presence of the Great I AM, who has been present in David in the Person of the Holy Spirit since the moment he received Christ as his Lord and Savior. It is that Person of the Trinity who has taken up residence and empowered David to capture the hearts and minds of those students in marvelous and compelling ways and who also gave

David the gifts of teaching and encouragement. It is because of that latter gift that he uses the second implication of "greatness" to enable those young folks to realize that they, too, possess the capacity to become as great as they have a desire to be. They are told that every person ever born on earth has had a purpose for being, and those who fail to discover that purpose will never truly be content or fulfilled.

I was greatly moved and highly impressed by David's abilities the first time I ever heard him speak at a men's retreat. His message that "Talk is Cheap" resonated very profoundly within me and confirmed what I had heard time and time again from some very wise people, "Small people talk about other people, greater people discuss ideas, but the greatest of people talk about their Lord and His work in their life." David's message focused on his humble testimony of mediocrity in scholastics, his eventual despair and his search for the true purpose of his life. It confirmed for me what I had already known from God's Word where the apostle Paul wrote: "Brothers and sisters, think of what you were when you were called. Not many of you were wise by human standards; not many were influential; not many were of noble birth. But God chose the foolish things of the world to shame the wise; God chose the weak things of the world to shame the strong. God chose the lowly things of this world and the despised things — and the things that are not — to nullify

the things that are, so that no one may boast before him."
(1 Corinthians 1:26-29) NIV.

Since that time, more than a decade ago, I have been privileged to financially support Talk is Cheap, to lift David and the ministry up in prayer and be his mentor in a deeper walk through God's Word. Though the dissimilar length of our respective years on Earth and disparate years of education might divide others, our union in Christ has made us equals in spirit and also at that eternally significant place where all who are saved by grace stand shoulder to shoulder and heart to heart on level ground at the foot of Calvary's Cross.

I congratulate my brother David on this, his first published work, and I pray that it will enable you to both seek and know the ULTIMATE GREATNESS and to appreciate the inward, potential, God- ordained greatness in yourself and others.

Soli Deo Gloria

Charles (Chuck) Hammond McGowen, MD

PREFACE

As founder of, and speaker for, Talk is Cheap, Inc. I have the opportunity to impact, and often initiate a change for the better in our youth, as well as in the lives of staff and academic leaders. As TIC has grown, so has the overall reach of that change, from my hometown, to statewide, national, and most recently international, something I never imagined at its inception.

Having reached out to more than 500,000 students to date, why did I feel the need to extend the message to literary form? Because young people are our future, because my goal has always been to build strong boys and girls rather than rebuild men and women, and because if in addition to speaking to that great a number of people, each of them had access to stories beyond those I was able to share with them in one brief encounter and perhaps pass this book along to a family member or friend, or even keep it within reach to refer back to, imagine the change that would be possible.

When I began speaking publicly 28 years ago I couldn't have imagined where Talk is Cheap, Inc. would lead. Perhaps you can't imagine right now the change this book may bring about in you, or the greatness that has always existed in you since the day you were conceived.

THERE IS NO TESTIMONY
WITHOUT A TEST

I knew God had His hand in my life … I just didn't know why. Had the events in the early eighties never taken place, can I imagine my existence? Oh, I can imagine it! It would have been very short. My life was spared many times, and left unbridled; I would have run myself into the ground.

Growing up in Youngstown, Ohio, in a family that had a strong faith base, I didn't understand that it was not about religion, but about having a relationship with God. As a teen, I became obstinate toward my family's spiritual beliefs and began to drift. It didn't take long for my moral compass to go astray and by high school, I found myself on a completely different path than what my parents and family would have chosen for me.

Diagnosed with Attention Deficit Hyperactivity Disorder during my seventh grade school year, I remember an experience I had as an altar server that demonstrated how much I truly struggled with ADHD and how it fed my low self-esteem.

Back in the seventies, the Catholic Mass included an altar server ringing bells at set times and, in the case of a Catholic funeral sacrament celebration, the use of incense. Keep in mind that ADHD and difficulty focusing often go hand in hand, and obviously during those most sacred moments of Mass, one needs to be attentive. This presented a moment in time I would rather forget, one of me not only ringing those bells at the *wrong* time, but worse yet, walking out from the back of the sacristy with incense in full bloom, and standing at the casket only to have a priest look at me and tensely lip, "Not yet!" The moral of the story? Most kids struggling to gain control over their ADHD should probably not be altar servers. ☺

Over the years, countless experiences combined to form what I saw to be the train wreck of my life. I now like to reveal to people when I speak or teach, my hope that one day the term LD will no longer stand for Learning Disabled, but rather for Learning Differently. My apologies to the professionals who prefer the more clinical term, but please keep in mind that at the end of the day it all comes down to a kid who now carries that title.

Needless to say, not only did my self-image suffer, but so did my attitude. People who understand the dynamics and leadership roles of family give credence to the fact that the eldest is typically both the most mature and the most responsible. As oldest of four siblings, that was not the case for me, yet it wasn't until down the road that I realized I had not taken on my responsibilities as the first-born. This too nourished my issues of self-worth.

Flash forward to my senior year in high school. It was 1981, and I had been at the home of a friend who had been trying to share his recent choice to begin to grow in his faith again, news I not only wasn't ready for, but was instead offended by. It was later that night while walking home that I found myself reflecting on how I just didn't fit in anywhere — not even in my own home. I saw

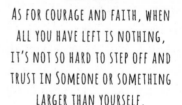

AS FOR COURAGE AND FAITH, WHEN ALL YOU HAVE LEFT IS NOTHING, IT'S NOT SO HARD TO STEP OFF AND TRUST IN SOMEONE OR SOMETHING LARGER THAN YOURSELF.

myself as the odd man out, the only one who had ADHD, a bad student who was always in trouble, and I was just tired of it all! What my friend said really made me think, and I realized that I didn't truly have a definitive future.

That night, I questioned why I was living. I contemplated suicide, and although this was not the first time I *had*, it *was* the first time I had a plan. I remember walking up a street in my neighborhood and mapping out in my mind how I would finally "fix" myself. It was right then, with all of this running through my mind that I had an "aha" moment. *God, if You are real, help me*, I pleaded. I knew my spiritual upbringing wasn't being practiced in my day to day life. Now all of a sudden, that divine need came to the forefront of my mind and heart and for the first time I really wanted something different. When you have nothing left, it's not so hard to step off and trust in Someone or something larger than yourself.

Three weeks later, there I was, a recent graduate dating my high school sweetheart (who has since 1985 been my beautiful bride), on the first of what would be many trips with her family to the Outer Banks. Along the way, we stopped in Virginia Beach to visit additional relatives. I would later discover that her Aunt Doris and Uncle Frank, mature believers in Christ, had only spent a bit of time with me and said, "This boy needs Jesus." Little did I know that it was on this family vacation that my testimony would present itself.

A rainy day at the beach provides a dilemma for someone like me; you see, with ADHD, one is not typically into the tedium of board games, so instead of joining the others, Susie and I visited a local laundromat. Truth be told, it was really just an excuse to get out of the games and possibly buy some beer and just hang out. God, however, had a different plan.

There we were, killing time in the last row of dryers when a man entered, walked past two rows of washing machines to approach me directly and said, "God told me to come in here and tell you that He loves you." Thinking either Bobby or Michael (Susie's brothers) had been behind this, I asked him which one had put him up to it. He just looked at me and said, "I don't know who Bobby or Michael are, but I do know God told me to come in here and tell you that He loves you." Still convinced it was a joke, I simply laughed. Repeating himself, the gentleman went on to tell me about his newfound faith, going on to say that if I asked God for help, He would help me too! He then handed me a Bible tract, (a short story/explanation of Jesus), and out he walked. I quickly shoved it in my pocket and even though I was uncomfortable, I had found him to be genuinely engaging and what he had said began to stir something within me. *If I asked God to help me, He would?* Asking God for help was something I had just done a few weeks earlier.

I didn't know who this man was, nor have I spoken to him since. Yet he had gone on to tell of his conversion to faith, sharing that had it not been for God answering his prayer, he would be dead. I would later attempt to read the "Full Gospel

Businessmen," pamphlet he had given me, but nothing that I read had made sense to me. Craziest of all, written on the back of the bible tract were three addresses. Two were of no real significance to me, but the third, well, it was a game changer… it was in Youngstown, Ohio!

It was upon my first day home that I set out to discover if the event itself and address were genuinely connected or if someone was just messing with me. I went in search of that property, and found that the address of the house listed in the back of the Bible tract sat 15 feet (literally directly across the street), from the friend's home that I'd left on that very night I'd contemplated ending my life. It was also the address of a devout evangelical Christian who was involved with a worldwide ministry, "The Full Gospel Business Men's Fellowship International," a fact which has since helped to add validity to a story some have questioned over the years, as the details just seemed too hard to believe.

Although I did eventually share what had happened with my family, at first it was too private to me. I was embarrassed. I was uncomfortable. I didn't really understand it. But once I'd put together some of the pieces of that trip in 1981, I figured it was time to come clean. The only place I'd ever done that was in a confessional, and so I sat down with a priest.

Having confessed and been transparent and honest for the first time, I walked out a new person. You see, I had done what

1 John 1:9 says, yet I didn't know what 1 John 1:9 *meant*.[1] "If we confess our sins, He is faithful and just and will forgive us our sins and purify us from all unrighteousness."[1] From that day on, I realized that God wasn't mad at me, God loved me; He knew me…it became a relationship.

I would go on to experience a number of spiritual "aha" moments over the next few years. Of course, there were many once I started reading my Bible, the acronym for which is: Basic Instructions Before Leaving Earth. You see, as author, speaker, and pastor, Anthony Campolo says, "If you did all the dos in the Bible, you wouldn't have time for the don'ts." The Bible is a love letter from God, and on a personal level, I had begun to develop a new appreciation.

One needs to understand that all of the signs we seek are addressed in His word, the Bible. The signs become answers and those answers are; Yes, No, and Wait! Sometimes the confusion in reading God's word stems from reading it from our own angle instead of His; Isa. 55:8,[2] "For My thoughts are not your thoughts, neither are your ways My ways." It would then be a safe option to pray as Jesus prayed; Luke 22:42[3] – saying, "Father, if You are willing, remove this cup from Me; yet not My will, but Yours be done." So, to a God follower I

---

1   1 John 1:9 (New American Standard)

2   Isa. 55:8

3   Luke 22:42

would encourage you to let your agendas or signs sit at His feet and be patient and wait. When God wants you to get something, you will!

To my friends reading this who do not subscribe to a faith-based solution to your wish for signs, it does not change how God feels about you! He doesn't play spiritual hide and seek. The Bible says in John 3:16 that God loved, God gave, and we must believe. Maybe the sign you seek will bring you right to the only One who can give it! My personal relationship with Jesus only became such because I ran out of me. Once I was out of the way, Jesus revealed Himself; just what He said, He is; "I am the Way, and the truth, and the life; no one comes to the Father but through Me."

HE HAS BROKEN
MY TEETH WITH GRAVEL

Just four years after that life-changing vacation, Susie and I were married, and a few years beyond that, we became parents to our two children, Courtney Lynn and David Michael. Employed at the time in sales of office equipment, I had also been serving as a volunteer youth pastor for three years at a Youngstown area church. There, as well as anywhere else I was invited, I taught and spoke to youth.

It was in 1992 that I was at home doing a routine weight workout when a momentary drop of the bar would prove yet again that not only is there no testimony without a test, but would confirm that haste really does make waste!

With dinner on the table upstairs, intent on finishing one more set of bench presses, I missed the catch rack on the bench I was using, and as I let go of the straight bar, it dropped from a full overhead extension onto my face. At that time I had no idea just how bad it was, or how fortunate I was. You see, although the bar landed on my chin knocking out eight bottom teeth, cutting my face wide open, and completely shattering my lower jaw, it could have landed on my throat causing a crushed windpipe, a broken neck, or my death!

Few may relate to this, but whenever I get hurt, my reactive response is anger, and so immediately pushing the bar off of me and onto my upper body, I sat up as teeth began to fall out of my mouth. Although I'd been intending to install mirrors to observe my form, thankfully I hadn't yet and had no way of seeing just how bad my injury really was. As I threw the bar completely off of myself and stood up, some affected teeth laid inside my mouth, as more fell out. Imagine being me at this moment!

I will spare you the grisliest of details, but suffice to say that my basement was beginning to look like a scene from a horror movie. I walked upstairs to find my bride and children already seated at the dinner table ready to give thanks; problem was, I wouldn't be eating that night, or for the next eight weeks as it would turn out.

With my hands cupped around my face, I mumbled to Susie that I had knocked my teeth out. Her smiling response was to "quit messing around." It was when I took my hands away from my face that she turned sheet white as I would later find out that she was seeing what appeared to be another mouth within my chin.

Having asked her not to panic, but to call a friend of ours who was a dentist, I could hear her telling him in a shaken voice that I had knocked out all my bottom teeth while lifting. Unfortunately, because of my practical joking nature, our faithful friend assumed we were both kidding. When Susie realized he wasn't taking us seriously, she hung up and instead called her parents. To this day, I feel so bad that he was put in that position; all of my years of fooling around had caught up with me. Sorry, dear friend!

Susie's parents lived the closest and arrived first, and even from a phone call away, my mother, who was a nurse, advised me to lie down and try to stay calm until help arrived. Meanwhile, my bride was downstairs picking up my teeth scattered about the basement floor.

At this point, I still hadn't seen my face, and oddly enough, it didn't really hurt. Thank God for shock. Our children on the other hand, were another story. Little David Michael was still in a high chair and wasn't too sure what was going on, but

Courtney Lynn was old enough to understand that daddy was hurt and mommy was scared.

Much of the remainder of the event remains a blur, but I do recall hearing my father-in-law repeatedly say on the drive to the hospital…"Oh Dave, Oh Dave." I don't recall gaining much comfort from that, but I do remember thinking Geez, relax, I just knocked a few teeth out! Of course, he was seeing what I hadn't yet.

Rushed to St. Elizabeth's Hospital, while pulling up the emergency ramp, I saw another family friend who was also a dentist. He, I would later discover, was heading into the hospital for a meeting of the entire staff of department heads. With my teeth in hand, he instead immediately expedited my entry into the emergency room.

If you have ever had the pleasure of visiting an ER, you know that most who work there are much more calm than the patient. In my case, it was a good thing that cooler heads prevail, as the doctor got me in within a few minutes. Although much of the ER was in a mild state of disbelief and concern, I still hadn't mustered up enough nerve to actually see what I had done.

The next few hours were a flurry of family and loved ones coming and going as doctors and nurses cleaned up my wounds as best they could and scheduled me for surgery to repair the destruction to my face. It was only now that I was beginning to understand the extent of the damage I had caused myself.

My bottom teeth had acted like a cutting surface and as the bar caught just the edge of my jaw, had cut right through below my bottom lip. Neat, huh? My first surgery was to close up the second mouth the accident had created, no doubt to the great relief of many whom I'd imagined probably thought that where I was concerned, one mouth was certainly enough.

My second surgery attempted to save my teeth that had been knocked out — eight in all! While one was missing, my poor mother-in-law successfully found it while searching the basement. I remember having to remain awake for that procedure, and as the head of plastic surgery began to work on my face, my mentor and friend came into the room, held my foot and prayed. I didn't know it was him at first because most of my line of sight was blocked, but I could see his hand on my foot and in his other hand, a Bible, and an enormous peace came over me.

It wasn't until later that the events of the day came into clearer view, as perhaps you are noticing the pattern as well. Not everyone has the indulgence of all of the department heads present on staff at the hospital in an emergency such as mine. Yet the entire night went like that, the head of plastic surgery, the head of oral surgery, even my primary care physician was there. Once we started putting the pieces of this event together it was overwhelming.

For one brief, shining moment good news arrived. Although I had knocked out my bottom teeth, my mouth appeared not to be broken. This news was short-lived as a 360° x-ray revealed that my jaw wasn't simply broken — it was shattered.

With Susie a stay-at-home mom and I the sole provider, our lives were about to get very interesting. We were both going to be stretched in ways we had never been at this point in our lives. Needless to say our marriage was about to be tested.

I faced surgery the following day to have my mouth wired shut to assist in the healing of my jaw. They were also going to put all of my bottom teeth back in place and hope for the best. With my mind running in 100 different directions, I did the only thing I knew would help — to have some quiet time and get my heart where it needed to be. I opened my Bible and took out my Our Daily Bread publication. With the issue a few days expired, I read the passage from the last day in February, a particularly long scripture reference that read:

Suspended Judgment

A mother wrote me that she had prayed daily for the safety of her son, but one day he was killed in an accident on the job. "For the past four years," she said, "I have been searching for the answer to why."

In another family, a sudden heart attack snatched Ray from Sylvia's side, leaving her to face life alone. When my wife and I visited her at the funeral home, we were met by a woman who was grieving but not asking God for an explanation.

What made the difference? Was it wrong for that mother to question God? Not at all! Sylvia too must have wondered about God's purpose in this tragedy. But from past experience she had come to know Him to be completely trustworthy. She could suspend judgment. "I don't need to ask why," she told us.

Jeremiah expressed much the same response in today's Scripture. Everything looked as if God had abandoned him, yet he said, "I hope in Him." His faith was no irrational, blind leap in the dark. Sound reasons based on experience backed it.

To suspend judgment when God is silent honors Him because it refuses to charge Him with being unjust. Those who express such faith are strengthened by God's Spirit and come to see how strong and good God really is. —D. De Haan

Though trials come, though fears assail,
Through tests scarce understood,
One truth shines clear—it cannot fail—
My God is right and good. —Hager

Those who bless God in their trials will be blessed by
God through their trials.

The scripture focused on Lamentations 3:1-24, with special emphasis on verse 16: "He has broken my teeth with gravel," the irony of which was not lost on me.

I was married. I had two children. I had just suffered permanent damage to my face and jaw. Initially I was angry, sad and confused, asking myself why we had to go through any of this. I remember at one time thinking, "Oh my gosh God, you really are letting all of this happen to me! A full-time, commissioned salesman and I'm going to have my mouth wired shut for eight weeks. It's funny. It's hilarious!'

What were my thoughts more regularly during those two months? I liken it to jumping from a perfectly good airplane with a parachute and it's overwhelming to think about all the mechanisms that are keeping you aloft. Instead, you just know you're floating and you're really grateful for that.

Miraculously, it was during those eight weeks with my jaw wired shut that I had two of my biggest months in sales at work. In addition, many anonymous donors graciously came alongside us, one making our house payment, while others provided groceries, and even had meals sent to our home. My bride asked that I include this story, one among many that I hope will make you smile.

We had a dear friend who owned a pizza shop and wanted to bless my family with a few wonderful pies. On the first night of what he thought would be a nice treat, Susie was out shopping with her mom and our kids, and she knew she needed to arrive home before the pizza was delivered.

She instead returned to find that it was too late! She found me sulking in my recliner in the living room, and walking to the kitchen, said she couldn't believe her eyes. There sat the blender, an open pizza box, and a bottle of Coke. Yes. I had tried to blend a piece of pizza with Coke, thinking I could drink it through a straw! The blender got much use during those two months; I even blended kielbasa and sauerkraut. People have often asked how many pounds I lost. The answer is zero. With my jaw wired shut I lost zero pounds! Have I mentioned that I'm a type A personality, and at times a bit OCD?

Countless experiences and narratives could be shared in this chapter but it comes down to one thing. We had to let go because there was nothing we could do. The entire ordeal was out of our hands except for one integral piece...our attitude. It was obvious God was providing for us, but in addition to long-term, we were also concerned with the day-to-day.

Hands down, we knew God was meeting all of our needs, but we were still scared. We could however trust that all would be OK because we had already experienced so many miracles. Susie and I were literally coming to terms with the sentence from the devotional I had read the morning of my surgery: "Those who bless God in their trials will be blessed by God through their trials."

TAKING A RISK

Since being married in 1985, my wife and I have been involved in a couples ministry every year. As we became more a part of the couples study fabric, Susie and I became more enmeshed with the teaching side of this group. I, however, had a conflict. I had a secret that was killing my marriage…and ruining me.

I could fix it. No one needed to know my personal business, and I intended to keep it that way. God and Susie had other ideas. Our leadership team met on Sunday night to begin preparations for a couple's retreat. My wife and I had been invited to be one

I HAD A SECRET THAT WAS KILLING MY MARRIAGE...AND RUINING ME.

of the couples who would share our own personal struggles in marriage and how together, we overcame those struggles.

The problem for me of course was choosing a topic. Knowing only that there was no way our theme would unearth my secret, on the evening we were asked to make a choice I was teaching youth group and couldn't be with my wife. In my absence, Susie chose the subject matter of anger management issues. She had set me up...but in a good way. You see, my anger was transforming me from a protector to a predator with my wife, a fact of which I'm not proud. I was two people. I was this guy who everyone knew as crazy and fun, yet I was also this stranger that NO one was allowed to know. That secret was destroying me, my marriage, and my family. Little did my proposed audience know that mine was the secret sin of rage.

After preparing our presentation and believing we were ready, we were required to have a dry run presentation for the team. Having done it twice, we were still being told, "I know that's not your talk," by the pastor who not only lead the couple's group from our church, but more importantly had known me since I rededicated my life to Christ in 1981.

After telling the truth in a confessional, I was attending anything and everything that had to do with Jesus. I went to Mass, but still wanted more. My sisters were at the time attending a Protestant church's youth program and attending a Sunday school class that met at someone's home. It was my thought that you had to go to church to speak to God, and yet, despite finding it a little weird, I was hungry and wanted to know more and so I went.

The first encounter I had with the man who would become my mentor, my friend, and a spiritual leader in my life, was amazing. He seemed to make the Bible verses that he taught come alive, seem practical, and most importantly, personal. With my sisters, I walked away that day thinking, I'm not sure what that was all about, but I want more! On that very day, this man became an instrumental cog in my spiritual wheel, and to date, that has never changed. His story was similar to mine, except he really did almost die as the result of a horrific car accident about which he said, "It was the only way God could get my attention." I found it confusing that despite permanent injuries as a result of the accident, he has joy!

Few knew the extent of my anger issues; I tried to keep it under the radar. The truth is that rage is one step before murder. "One of these days, you're going to do something you're going to regret," the pastor said and once again sent Susie and me off to work on our talk.

We gave our best attempt, all the while avoiding the exposure of my secret. Literally the night before we were to speak, we still didn't have it finished. The retreat weekend would begin Friday night and go on throughout the day on Saturday, with our slot scheduled for first thing Saturday morning. We worked until midnight continuing to guard what was restricted while trying to put together the missing pieces. As I have stated, God and Susie had other intentions with this talk, and early Saturday morning I awakened from a very troubling dream. It was a vivid recall from a time in my life when I witnessed someone else in a rage-filled moment, and I remember feeling terrified and vulnerable, not unlike the feeling my own bride and children must have felt when they saw that in me.

They saw that in me. Suddenly, I knew exactly what to do! Talk *is* cheap. The couples in that room that morning needed to see, not hear. The old saying, "The truth hurts," is an understatement, but there is another saying about the truth – that it will set you free, and set me free, it did, at the great expense of my pride.

Speaking to 30-plus couples with a total of approximately 70 people, most of whom I knew, the day was for the most part unscripted. Before we spoke that morning, and without really even explaining the unfolding events to Susie, I asked a few guys to round up some magazines, books, newspapers, and a table. I asked them to place the table up front with the magazines and such scattered messily about on it, making sure the table was in front of where Susie and I would be speaking and in plain sight of all in attendance. I was to address my wife, and then re-enter after less than a minute as though I was returning at the end of the work day.

I had explained myself to the lead couple of the retreat and they told me that if that was what I felt I needed to do, then go for it. In my mind, although I knew I was going to actually pretend how I would act in a moment of rage, even I didn't know it would actually become one. We were introduced as the next couple giving a talk on the subject of anger and people politely clapped at our introduction as we approached the podium. With Susie still unaware of the turn of events about to happen, and me not yet having spoken a word, I walked away, and looking at her as though we were already in the middle of a discussion, an angry voice came from within me. I don't care what you do today, I said, as that irate tone rose from me; all I ask is that you please clean up this table before I get home from work.

Walking towards one of the few doors leading out of the room where we were all meeting, I slammed the door as hard as I could to make sure she knew I was serious. I was unaware that the people who knew me had begun to laugh, thinking I was horsing around. The facilitator of the weekend however, stood up and motioned that it was not a joke. Because this was all off-the-cuff, I stood for a few seconds with no real idea of what I'd do next.

Just then, that old self, "secret Dave," took over. I walked back into the room and greeted Susie pleasantly; role playing that I had just arrived home from a long day at work. I then noticed that the table remained untouched. Focusing on the uncompleted task, I asked her what the one thing was that I had asked to have completed before I had left, to which she replied, "To straighten up the magazines."

Truly caught up in the moment, no acting was taking place as the embers of my mood flamed, progressing rapidly from agitation to anger, and soon...fury. With both me and Susie unaware of the direction in which the "talk" and the mood were traveling, in one move I wiped the table clear of the magazines, raging on and ripping into her and then slowly walking to the podium. I am telling you it was absolutely a "God thing," as none of it had been in my head. The look in her eyes was one I'd seen before; it was one of terror and vulnerability. I waited a moment and introduced myself and my wife, and announced that the topic of our talk was anger.

Barely able to compose myself, I wept throughout the entire talk. At one point, my wife literally rubbed my back and said to me, "We can stop if you want." I replied no, and we continued. It was the most embarrassed, exposed, and most vulnerable I had ever felt, and yet at the same time, also the most relieved. It was common for couples to retreat to hotel rooms to discuss the "talk." Returning to a shocked, tense room however, this time, everyone was instructed to stay and told that the Kohout's would stand in the back should anyone want to speak with them, or have us pray for them.

I was mortified. I wanted to run and hide. You see, prior to the couples retreat, most of the people in that room knew David Kohout as a more of a comedian, that is until they saw this side of me. Aside from my wife and children, the only other person who had seen that side of me since coming to Christ was my mentor. How, after acting the way I just had, could I look someone in the eye, speak with them, or even more absurdly... pray for them? Not to mention, who in their right mind would want to talk to me or have me pray for them? Then it happened!

People began getting up and coming towards the back. The first couple, Susie and I knew well. The husband was a much larger man than I and I was convinced the only reason he was coming towards me was to let me have it. He never knew this of me; I felt that I had to have let him down. I was sure it was now his turn to set me straight.

They walked toward us, his wife hugged mine, and then, this bear of a man hugged me, at one point enveloping me so intensely that my feet left the ground, as he wept into my shoulder. He cried so hard for a brief second that it was awkward, yet it was then that I realized, they too struggled. I had never experienced anything like this! As he began to regain control, with tears in both his and his wife's eyes, they thanked us and began to walk away. That's when, looking past them, we saw the line. A procession of couples had formed, many crying, holding each other…all of them waiting to speak with us. I was so confused — so shocked that anyone would want to speak to me after what they had just learned.

I had read a book entitled "Go the Distance," in which there was one sentence that summed up the events of that morning. "Brokenness is a fundamental, non-negotiable prerequisite for all that God is calling you to do."

I didn't know it then, but as our couple's team leader would later point out, the line that had formed after we spoke, was the grieving line for a person who had died. That person was me. They were acknowledging how fallen at times they were in their own marriages, but that quitting wasn't an option. They were waiting to encourage and thank us. It was all so overwhelming.

I would like to say that from that time on I have never struggled again with my temper, but that would be a lie. What I can say is that I have never been that man since. The secret is no more. I openly talk about that struggle and many others and I find that by talking about them they have less power over me. I can also say that my issues with rage are almost completely gone in comparison to before that day. Would I urge you to have the courage to come forth and expose the lie perhaps you so closely guard? No. Not until you are so sick of it destroying you and those you love that you no longer care about the consequences — only the breakthrough.

As bad as it was, as uncomfortable as it was, as embarrassing as it was, I'd kept going, and in the end, I WON. If we don't come clean with what we keep secret, that secret is going to destroy us. I had managed the "talk." I had bared my secret sin. I had connected with couples on a level more intimate than I could have imagined.

I am not a historian, but I have heard of an account where those who took an overseas journey by ship were encouraged, once they reached the new land, to burn the ships in order not to be tempted to go back.

If I have learned anything about risk, it is this. Life = Risk. If you are ever really going to accomplish something that will stand the test of time, you have to take the risk. I am grateful to Susie for taking the risk to pick anger as our topic. I am grateful to the couples team and leaders who encouraged us to keep working at our "talk" when we thought it was done. I am most grateful to God who loves us just the way we are, yet too much to leave us that way!

4   THE TRUE PROVIDER

That earlier couple's retreat was more than likely a defining moment for my employers, from whom I received the following message that would change everything for me.

"We're not firing you...but you have to quit." An email message that was certain to alter the landscape of my family's life as we knew it. Steve and Kathy Blakeman had witnessed firsthand how God was using my life to impact the lives of others and they felt that by allowing me to continue to work for them and Valley Office that they would have been interfering with God's plan for my life. Not ones for confrontation, they had heard me speak at numerous venues as well as at a recent couples retreat, and opted to send that fateful email knowing in their hearts that I was destined for more than sales.

My employers from 1985 through 1999, with a relationship that spanned 14 years, found the prospect of me moving on both sad and daunting. With it being all that I'd known, I was blessed to be one of their top producers and it was difficult for me to walk away.

Sharing the words of my employer with my wife, "You can't quit," she said. We were comfortable with our lifestyle, and with two children, would be left without insurance. At the time, I was doing a personal study in a resource called "Experiencing God," by Dr. Henry Blackaby. The portion I was studying in this workbook was unit seven: "The Crisis of Belief." Page 149 had a heading that read "Actions Speak Louder than Words," and a sentence below it would challenge my heart and provide me with the name of our organization, Talk is Cheap. The sentence read, "When God invites you to join Him and you face a crisis of belief, what you do next reveals what you believe about God. Your actions speak louder than words." That was it...what we were experiencing was a crisis of belief that required faith and action. Within six months, I had quit my job. I would remain unemployed for no more than one week and as it would turn out, God provided insurance that included vision and dental!

I approached my pastor at the time, explaining what I wanted to do with youth, and he referred me to Bob Stauffer, with whom I'd met previously regarding the inception of a youth center. Bob had recently stepped down as a senior pastor in the Youngstown area to offer leadership to the Fellowship of Christian Athletes. I recall contacting him and briefly explaining my reason for calling. He indicated that in light of his recent career change, I should give him a few weeks and then call back. There I was in full-blown crisis mode, attempting to figure things out, and "wait" is never an answer I like to hear. As respectfully as possible, I offered up breakfast, lunch, dinner, or a midnight snack, stressing that I really needed to meet with him. My persistence was acknowledged and rewarded with a lunch meeting the very next day.

As long as I live I will never forget that exchange. We met at a restaurant across from Youngstown State University, and following the initial hello, he said, "Let's grab some food and sit down and you can tell me what's on your mind." I was so excited I spoke at wind gust levels! Finally, here was someone who could hear what I had on my heart and offer direction accordingly. Here was a lifeline of hope.

I'm not sure how long I shared but when I was finished, I looked at him and enthusiastically asked him what he thought. His response crushed me. "Well, after hearing everything you have on your heart, I must admit, I have no idea what you are talking about," he said. In stunned disbelief I sat there and then mustered up the words…which part? Staring back at me, he said, "All of it." He then gently went on to reiterate all that I had said, explaining that I couldn't possibly do ALL of it. Clarifying that it would take me in too many directions, he added that not every one of my plans coincided with the bigger picture. Then he made a statement that was life changing. "David, you have to take good and lay it at the altar of best," he said. Now, *I* was the one confused. For the past 16-plus years of my life I felt as though I'd been a decent communicator, and yet with one sentence, "I have no idea what you are talking about," he had completely derailed me from what I thought was an awesome plan. That design was to approach some local business people who love God and kids and who are blessed with financial resources, and begin putting together a plan on how we could best impact the teens of our communities.

Bob explained to me that taking such an approach without first having a plan would be business suicide. Assuring me that while I might get a small check and a pat on the head, "That would be about it," he said. He instead encouraged me to devise a plan before meeting with any potential donors.

To say I was deflated, is to say the ocean is "kinda" big. I sat there, utterly baffled as to what was my next move. Apparently my demeanor wasn't lost on Bob, who then offered to have me join him and some colleagues on a leadership trip they would be attending in just a few days. After indicating that sales for me had been modest for the past few months, and that I couldn't afford a trip just then, I was amazed at his response. "Let us encourage you on your journey; good things are coming," he said. The trip, on which I humbly accepted the offer to join him, was life changing; equally so, was meeting the other men on it. Unbeknownst to me, they were sizing me up to be their first hire under Bob's leadership of the local FCA office. He asked me to join FCA, telling me, "You'll get to be on the front line of delivering a message of hope." I took him up on his offer, and remained with FCA for four years. For nearly a year of that time, I also ran The Teen Center, which was a 501(c) (3). Through it all, I met some amazing people, and we got to do a lot of remarkable things in the name of ministry.

In addition to having supplied some office space for FCA, Jim and Kim Poma also had a love for God and kids. As a result of our mutual passions, we began collaborating on how we could impact a greater number of teens in our community. We agreed that having a youth center where kids could go to hang out and have fun in a safe environment would be a great option. The Teen Center I mentioned earlier was the first facility we initiated. Still employed part-time by FCA, budgets were down and my position was the first eliminated. Because the Poma's saw my talents and gifts more clearly than I did, they opened up additional space in their building to allow us to run that youth facility as well as blessing it financially, providing me the opportunity to continue to grow in the area of serving youth.

Much more significant than their donation of warehouse space, the Poma's graciously gave of their time, treasures, and talents to make that youth center a reality. If by now you haven't noticed, the pattern continues.

Every time I am down to nothing, God is up to something. I didn't mention this earlier, but when I sat down with Bob and discussed my visions of grandeur, a meeting with the person I had planned to approach did come to pass, however it was on the leadership trip I

EVERY TIME I AM DOWN TO NOTHING, GOD IS UP TO SOMETHING. GOD'S GOT A PLAN…HE DOESN'T MAKE MISTAKES.

attended with him and his companions. One of the men was the son of a prominent philanthropic community member and the very person I had planned to approach just a few weeks earlier. Joining the group at the conference at Willow Creek Church in Barrington, Illinois, my world was rocked. I would liken it to visiting a small rural church out in the middle of nowhere, and then being dropped in the middle of the Vatican. Pulling up to it, I bawled. Until then all I could see were little trees. I had to take a step back to see the forest.

I love to repeat a statement Bob used to make frequently; "If you didn't know any better, you'd think God knew what He was doing (wink, wink)!" Well to say God did, would be an understatement. All my worrying and fretting and complaining, and things ended up working out better than I could have hoped or dreamed.

So tell me...what are your hopes? What are your dreams? Who sabotaged your dreams? Who crushed your hopes? As I write this, please know that life isn't a bowl of cherries for me either, but I've come to understand that life is easier with God than without Him. I love when people want to drag me into their arguments with their strong beliefs against what I have experienced. But that's just it; I experienced it! I'm sorry they haven't, but with a gun to my head, you couldn't talk me out of what I believe because truthfully, no one talked me *into* it! I would love to be able to help you "see it," but honestly, seeing the things that God has done is kind of like "Where's Waldo." You look and see nothing, but then as you settle down and begin to take in the entire picture, BOOM, there it is. There He is!

The purpose of this chapter is not to convince you of anything. The Greek philosopher Socrates said, "I cannot teach anybody anything, I can only make them think." You know full well that this is not the first time you have heard such detailed accounts of how God did something. The problem lies not in the accounts, but in the 18-inch distance. Author Maria Durso wrote in her book, *From Your Head to Your Heart*, "The change you look for is 18 inches away." Connecting the heart and the mind can be a lifetime struggle. Fortunately for me, my faith journey began early and some of the secular mindset being taught in high school and college did not have an opportunity to change my non-negotiables to maybes.

If what I just shared in this chapter has touched your heart, perhaps right where you sit you could pray as simple a prayer as I did in 1981, saying, "God, if you are real, help me. Open my eyes to Your spiritual truth, connect my heart and mind, and help me to believe."

If you have prayed that prayer, please email me and share what happened over the next few hours, days, and week. Notice, I didn't say weeks? He won't take weeks. The fact that you have this book in your hands is proof positive that God loves you and has not quit trying to establish that relationship between you and Him. I'm telling you; life is brighter, smells better, and sounds clearer when the One who formed you in your mother's womb (Psalm 139:13) begins to permeate your heart and mind. You'll see, and please don't forget to email me at David@SITPOG.com.

IT'S NOT IMPORTANT WHAT OTHERS THINK...UNLESS IT'S YOUR WIFE AND KIDS

5

ave I been reflective on the positive changes in my life and the impact they had on my family? Yes. Keep in mind I have amassed a journal of more than 400 pages spanning from 1999 to the present. The truth is…I feel like I got a second chance…as a Christian, and in my marriage, not to mention that I could have lost both of my kids later in life. Without having changed the way I was living my life, there may have come a time when they would have said…hey, you're not the guy you said you were.

Having read the thoughts my children chose to share for this book on their lives with their dad brought to mind a gift I had asked for upon my 50th birthday. I told my kids that if they really wanted to bless me, they could write me a letter.

I admit at first, I was a little afraid to read them, but those letters became keepsakes. These excerpts shared by my wife and children for the purposes of this book are sure to be as well.

Susie on her husband

My husband has addressed much of both his past and our history in previous chapters; issues that involved and affected us both, from his testimony, to his then newfound dedication to Christ, our family, and his temper.

Chapter five is my chance to share my perspective. Having met our junior year in high school, Dave and I started dating at 16, doing a lot of the typical things teenagers do. It was pretty much all about us! At the age of 18, when Dave joined my family on vacation, little did we know that that trip would forever change us.

While Dave had been searching for something new and real in his life, I thought that things were just fine. That encounter however, started a journey of searching for God in a whole new dimension. As a result of that quest, my husband started going to church more, eventually joining a new church, and even a Bible study. Although I did go along for an entire year, I admit I wasn't truly into it. One day, Dave told me that if I didn't get my life straight with the Lord we were not to have a future. Little by little, I began to understand what he had already known and experienced; that it's not about the head knowledge with the Lord…it's about a relationship with Him.

And so we started to grow together spiritually. Fast forward to marriage and the birth of our two children; I was a stay-at-home mom, Dave worked very hard and found great success in his job. Life was good.

Admittedly, there were times when Dave would show his temper, usually when under stress. Never wanting to embarrass him, I would just deal with it and keep it to myself. Although those times weren't on a regular basis, when Dave did get mad, he tended to go off the deep end, usually leaving and regrouping afterward. After many years of this, I decided I couldn't do it for the rest of my life. I had mentally packed my bags and thought about taking our children and leaving him on more than one occasion.

The couples retreat at which we addressed the topic of anger was not only the start of restoration for our marriage, as it turned out, many of the couples in that room dealt with the same issue — that secret sin of rage. Since that time God has changed Dave from the inside out; he is a wonderful husband and father whose goal is to serve me — and he does!

It was very clear that God was doing something very special in Dave's life and that he had a call in his life to speak to teenagers. We received a lot of confirmations through other people who agreed with this decision.

Fast forward once again, and you can only imagine my reaction when Dave told me he was quitting his job and trusting in the Lord for the next one. Who does that? A man of great faith, that's who. Within two weeks Dave was again working, and once again, life was good. Dave loved his job with FCA, and I was now working part time. When he lost his job with FCA due to lack of funding, my security once again went with it.

My husband once told me that God, not his employer, was our Provider. I have never forgotten that. I don't always have the faith I need to trust in that, but I know in my heart it's true.

Nine years ago we started Talk is Cheap, and what an emotional roller coaster ride it has been! I guess I never thought we would be in ministry; certainly not at the beginning of our marriage. I figured we would just have traditional jobs, save for retirement, raise our children and have no worries; I was pretty naïve.

There is a study by Henry Blackaby called "Experiencing God," in which his states, "God knows what we need, and He can lay that need on anyone's heart He chooses." His words literally jumped off the page in what was a "WOW" moment to me. Dave and I have never asked for money. We've never held a fundraiser. Yet, God continually uses people to bless us with what we need. It's not always easy...I still struggle with trusting God for finances, but He constantly proves me wrong. He is in control and He does provide our every need. So when I'm worried about finances I often revisit that passage, and it helps me to remember that I'm not alone, that God cares, and that He will provide.

As I watch Dave get up and speak and pour into the lives of teenagers I am always amazed by the gift God has given him! He speaks truth into their lives. In most of his assemblies, you can hear a pin drop. Kids really dial in and believe in what he is saying. They trust him. I have been at the conclusion of numerous assemblies where the line is so long with kids clamoring for a few private minutes with Dave to tell him their story, and I am touched many times, often to the point of tears. I know Dave is being used greatly to help the youth of this world.

Looking back, I believe we have benefited significantly by Dave's leap of faith to quit his job way back when. As a result, our children have grown in their faith as well. There is a bigger purpose in the world than being fat and happy... it's about giving and reaching out...finding a need and filling it. I'm excited to see what God is going to do with TIC in the future!

I cannot tell you how many times I've been out shopping and have had a cashier see my last name and ask if my husband is a speaker. When they hear that he is, the response is always the same. They tell me he visited their school, and that they love him. My response as well is always the same. I ask them *what am I standing in the presence of*, to which the reply is GREATNESS…and a big smile. It always blesses me. Some of these kids have been out of school for 10 plus years and they still remember the message…that's pretty awesome!

Courtney Lynn on her dad

My dad's testimony and relationship with God has greatly impacted me, my life, and that of our family, for the better. As the leader of our family, he made a point to make sure we were at church regularly. He always set a great Godly example — we prayed before every meal, he frequently played Christian music in the house/car, had us pray together as a family, and was always very supportive for all of us. Something I specifically remember was every Christmas he set aside time for us to read the Bible as a family and reflect upon the true meaning of Christmas, something I'm sure most families don't do.

During my middle school years I didn't like how strict my parents were with us. We were limited in what we could watch on TV, what kind of music we could listen to, and we were never allowed to sleep over friends' houses. At that time I'm sure I gave both of my parents attitude because "they never let me do anything", but now as an adult looking back, I understand why they parented the way they did. It wasn't because they wanted to make us miserable; it's because they wanted to protect us and keep us as pure as possible in what can be a horribly corrupt world. Since my dad had lived as part of that world and was actively involved in it during his childhood and into his teenage years, he specifically knew what was out there and didn't want his kids to be exposed to it. So, despite frustration then, I now laugh because I'm sure I'll raise my kids very similarly to how I was raised. That brings to mind a quote we had on our refrigerator which said something along the lines of, "When you're old enough to realize your parents were right, you'll have kids of your own who think you're wrong." I remember he would reference that a lot when we were younger, and now I know why.

I can say without a doubt that if my dad had not gotten serious in his relationship with God, not only would neither I, my brother, nor my mom be who we are today, we'd be an entirely different family; perhaps not even still together as a family unit. My dad set a great example for me as his daughter by how he treated my mom, which in turn set a standard for what I look for in a potential partner. I can genuinely say that I have an amazing, incredibly loving and supportive dad. He has always been there for all of us, and did a great job setting a Godly example for our whole family.

DAVID MICHAEL ON HIS DAD

It seems that the older I get the more I realize that there isn't a day, in fact not even an hour most days, that I'm not doing or thinking of something that reminds me of my dad. I am my father's son and I'm beginning to realize it more and more with age.

All my life, my dad has planted seeds in me; seeds of motivation, seeds of love, seeds of a servant heart, seeds of caring, seeds of leading, and most of all, the seeds of forgiveness and Christ. I've learned that the leader in him cares, loves, motivates and serves and I am now seeing that I have been made to do all of those things. I've also begun to see how much of a role Christ plays in my everyday life and recognize the importance of forgiving people. In this past year alone I've noticed how much more I've come to him for advice or called on him for help. It's rubbed off on me and I now know why I think and act the way that I do. Both his testimony and his life changes have affected my life entirely. I've seen the good, the bad and the ugly of him and he would admit it! I've seen my dad lose his patience and/or his temper but the amazing thing is that I've seen him bounce back and reflect on his actions and take full responsibility, apologizing for them. Not many people can say their father knelt down in front of them or alongside them after disciplining them to simply apologize and let them know they still love you.

I've met people all over who recognize my last name and have told me my dad spoke to them. That's been the case for me ever since grade school. Imagine going to a party in middle or high school and having someone come up to you and tell you that your dad made them cry in their school assembly or health class just a few hours ago. It was both a great feeling and uncomfortable as I was trying to have a good time and most likely not have my parents find out about it. I just LOL'd…but it's the truth!

But truly, my dad's talk and testimony were reaching both young and old all over the map! High school was interesting for me and I knew it all along, so much so that I never wanted to do anything that could get me into so much trouble that it would jeopardize or risk TIC or what my dad stood for. I wasn't always the greatest kid but out of respect I never wanted to harm what my dad did in schools. I knew close friends he'd helped and I watched them transform because of him and Christ through him.

My dad was and is always there for me. I know no matter what it is I can always call him and at my very first question he'll stop whatever he's doing to try and help. My sister, mom and I come first to him and that's always been a blessing we have that many people don't have in their lives. You'll never meet a more caring man. Come to think of it, there's no one in my life who's been as influential as he has been for me. He's always encouraging me and he's always in my corner every step of the way.

6
CHRIS SUTTON:
WHAT'S YOUR EXCUSE FOR
NOT DOING SOMETHING?

N
o matter how long you live, don't ever forget me," he said.
And so, I made a promise. Every time I speak...*every* time,
I share his story because I vowed that I would.

I didn't know Christopher Sutton very well as a kid... he was one of a hundred plus kids with whom I was familiar. Although he and his family were members of Trinity Fellowship, where I was at the time serving as Youth Pastor, my mind was overwhelmed with a full-time job, a young family, and running a youth ministry. The reason he stood out that one evening at a YMCA sleepover was because of all the kids to whom I gave an instruction, he was the only one who, before I could even finish, did the very thing I had directed them not to do. Don't run, I had said. What did Chris do? He ran. I remember thinking to myself... what the heck is wrong with this kid?

Now, I don't hear God's voice any more than you do. Sure, I've heard these "nudges" for many, many, years and always thought... ahhh...it's just me thinking it. But this time, I felt like God said... "YOU were the exact same kid." As we would later come to realize, Chris and I were a lot alike. He, too, had attention issues. As his mom would say, "Chris had much more of an interest in people than in school." He had some self-control issues. He was at times inappropriate with his comments or at least the timing thereof, but he had a heart of gold. It was hard not to like him. Although I didn't mind saying goodbye to Chris that first night, it would be less than three weeks later that his mother would call me to say that her son was in trouble.

The son of Eric and Judy Sutton, Chris was a promise from God, in his mom's words. Explaining that at a time when she and her husband were parents to five-year-old Kyle, they found themselves unable to have additional children and had begun to explore the prospect of adoption.

Sitting beneath a tree following a retreat, she said she heard God tell her that she would have another child. Feeling more convinced than ever that her future would in fact hold an addition to their family, she said she soon afterward received a call from her pastor regarding the possibility of a private adoption. As would later reveal itself, the expectant woman from whom she would adopt Chris, had a due date that fell exactly nine months from that of the retreat after which she'd heard those prophetic words.

Chris knew about God and had a relationship with Him from an early age, according to his mom, who said that there was a confidence placed in him. Chris was 13 years old, in the seventh grade in Boardman Schools, a suburb of Youngstown, Ohio, and a member of my youth group when doctors found a tumor the size of a small football wrapped around his aorta and spine. Yes, Chris was in fact in trouble.

First treated at a local hospital, Chris was moved to a more experienced hospital in the Cleveland area, where surgeons operated and removed more than eighty percent of the growth. Afterwards, he underwent radiation and chemotherapy, which subsequently caused his hair loss. Knowing he would lose his hair, Chris had a hairdresser come to the house and cut his hair to look like mine, enjoying the amusement all too briefly as his would fall out soon afterward.

It was upon Chris' first time returning to youth group, that he arrived with his friend Nicholas Rowe, who attended Lowellville Schools. Both young men were bald. When asked about his new 'do,' Rowe said, "If my best friend's going to be bald, so am I."

When I speak of Chris, I ask the students to whom I'm presenting if they'd like to have a friend like Nick, and then encourage them to *be* that friend. Chris had such a tender spirit, such a gentle heart. It was, in fact, at youth group that he once heard of a girl who couldn't afford a prom dress. Chris purchased one for her. That girl was Heather Ramsey, who is now a teacher in Poland, Ohio and whose students she says are witness to the strength of one young man whose life here may have ended but whose message carries on.

Following a three-year remission during which Chris was able to return to school, his cancer resurfaced, this time in his spine and eventually, traveling to his brain. Chris once asked me if he was going to die. I told him we're all going to die someday and asked him how he wanted to finish his race. It was during

Chris' second bout with cancer that I would witness how he intended to cross the finish line of his life.

Chris' fellow students at Boardman High School began to see the gravity of his situation and although still the same high school students, suddenly pecking order and prestige no longer mattered. The BHS students created a banner; one that even community members stopped in to sign and it was then delivered to the hospital by the Boardman High School cheerleaders. Far too large to hang in his room, the banner was suspended instead in the hall of the hospital. According to Chris's mom, by that time, her son no longer had use of his legs and was unable to stand on his own. His father held him up so he could read every message. That banner demonstrated the love and concern so many had for him and how he had touched their lives. For Chris, his family and friends, and even for the hospital staff, it was a moment in time that transcended the darkness of his cancer. Chris' final hospital stay would be for 52 days.

Chris was way beyond his years. He called me one day and asked if I could come to his house. He told me, "I want you to hear a song I want for my funeral." The song was "He's My Son," by Mark Schultz. He had also created a PowerPoint of photos of himself from birth to present, and went on to ask me to speak at his funeral; I told him I'd be honored. Sharing that Chris told her what he wanted in his casket, his mom said he stated that he wanted to wear his new black suit with his silver shirt. He wanted his Bible with the inscription "No fears, no regrets, just a future with a promise" on the cover to be laid on his chest, and that he wanted his sword in his hand. She said he had ordered the sword himself from a catalog because he had had a vision of it in his hand. The instrument represented the sword of the Spirit, part of the armor of God.

Hoping that people would ask what it was for, his mom, dad, and brother Kyle could share with people, "Above all, taking the shield of faith, wherewith ye shall be able to quench all the fiery darts of the wicked. And take the helmet of salvation, and the sword of the Spirit, which is the word of God." "Everything Chris did was a message," said his mom.

Because Chris was strong in the Lord, his mom said he was able to remain joyful throughout the two and a half years of his cancer battle. Always an encourager, cancer didn't rob him of that, she said. "Perfect love casts out all fear." 1 John 4:18. Chris always cared how his illness and death would affect others. There was a protection around Chris, according to his mom. She would share the story of a young girl who, during Chris' second cancer battle, would visit their home often, bring food for the family, and sit with Chris for long periods of time. The visitor would later write about him, his life, and his death, saying that at times, she wanted to leave but couldn't, as she felt God's presence in the room.

Chris' final days came to be while I was on a family vacation in Florida over the Thanksgiving holiday. University Hospitals in Cleveland had arranged for contemporary Christian singer/songwriter Michael W. Smith to call Chris the day after he had left the hospital. Upon calling, he was informed that Chris had slipped into a coma. The phone was held to his ear while Smith spoke to him, and afterward, to Chris' mom. I too called to speak with Chris, and as they held the phone to his ear, I spoke to him…telling him, Chris, I love you. I'm proud of you. I'll show your picture, I'll play your song, share your story and ask people what their excuse is for not doing something.

As the end of Chris' life grew imminent, there was concern that his sword wouldn't arrive in time. It was in fact delivered via FedEx the day before Thanksgiving. Chris' brother Kyle called me on Thanksgiving Day, 1999 to tell me that Chris had died. Chris was 17 years old.

As promised, I spoke at Chris' funeral, where it was very apparent God's spirit and anointing were in that sanctuary.

In his casket as he had wished, he held his inscribed Bible. The song "Not My Will," a song that Chris and a friend of his had sung together, would be sung by her alone that day.

Chris and I had always joked around saying…"You punk… if you beat me to heaven I'll see you again." Well, Chris did beat me to heaven, but his story here endures. Chris could have been a victim, yet instead, I had seen what a model patient he was.

That boy impacted my life. With every group to whom I speak, Chris and the way he chose to finish his race continues to make a difference. I was a kindred spirit to the young man placed in my youth group. God's got a plan…He doesn't make mistakes.

In the months following the death of their son, the Suttons cared for a family of children on weekends and would soon adopt eight-year-old Alyssa. Twenty years old at the time of this writing, she has attended community college, and lives locally. Kyle Sutton was a student at Mount Union at the time of Chris' illness and returned home to be with his family. A young adult making life decisions and facing the loss of his only sibling; for a time his faith was shaken, said his mom. Now 37, Kyle is

married and lives in Pittsburgh with his wife and two sons. He and Alyssa remain close and just as they do with me; memories of Chris and the manner in which he chose to finish his race remain with his family.

Chris, whom his mom said wanted to be a youth pastor like me, would be 31 today.

A Work In Progress

C hristopher Sutton is no doubt keenly aware that while his time here on earth was done, his work certainly was not. Because of both the impact he had on all who knew him and the promise I continue to honor, Chris' message continues to spread sixteen years beyond his passing. Countless students have been influenced by his story, as his life and death continue to inspire both them and me. Chris may have finished his race here, but his legacy endures through those of us who came to know him when he walked with us. Our finish lines are drawn.

The manner in which we embellish them along the way is up to us.

From the inception of Talk is Cheap, Inc., my intent and mission have never faltered. I want to set foot on every campus and tell every kid that they matter, that they are not a mistake,

I WANT KIDS TO LAY THEIR HEADS ON THEIR PILLOW AT NIGHT WITH LESS REGRET AND MORE HOPE.

they are not an accident, and that there is a purpose for their life. I want kids to lay their heads on their pillow at night with less regret and more hope.

Just as my resolve hasn't changed, neither has my initial perception of need right here at home. While I would like to spend all of my time in Ohio, words of greatness have spread, and brought me in touch with people along the way who have afforded me opportunities to impact kids globally. While my roots remain here, kids are kids and needs are needs. I go where I'm welcomed and I'm honored to do so every time.

My work and passion to help youth has spanned from the elementary to college campus and off the beaten path to assisting some who have made poor choices with dire consequences. Some of them have gone on to grasp the concept of greatness and found their way back. Others continue to struggle, as we all do as works in progress. It's never too late to make a change; never too late to ask for help. My former boss (and still to this day dear friend) always reminded me that as long as there is breath, there is hope.

While making the journey, as I've shared with you, my temperament has calmed, and although there are areas of discipline in my life that are at times not as they should be, my overall attitude toward life is considerably better. Again…life is a passage, during which the difference between winners and losers is quitting, and I aint quitting!!

I've bared my soul to some extent in what you've read here. My intent is not to convert anyone, but to provide food for thought. As you recall, I shared the words of Socrates, "I cannot teach anybody anything, I can only make them think."

And so I ask…has it made *you* think? How are you? How do you feel? Are you harboring stress? Are you holding onto a forgiveness issue? Is your child trying to get your attention because you're busy working to make ends meet? If the seed of greatness is in you…who do you think put it there? What are you going to do with it? How are you nurturing or protecting it, or is it slowly dying?

I ask of you; since life really is a journey, why wouldn't you at least consider asking Jesus to be a part of it? I have had the privilege of sitting and talking with financially wealthy people and more than once have heard them say, "I have had very little money and now have vast amounts of money, and given the choice, having vast amounts of money is way better!"

Likewise, I can say that I have had no relationship with Jesus, and now have a relationship with Jesus, and I can assure, having Him as a friend and savior is way better than not! His coming into my life didn't make me perfect, but from eternity's vantage point, my sins have, are, and will be forgiven. That can put some wind in your sails!

If you once called Him a friend but have grown cold and distant, remember that He didn't move; you did. Come back. He was never mad at you. You didn't let him down; you were never holding Him up!

Enough about me; let's talk about you. In all honesty, I don't care about your financial wellness, about your relationship statuses, etc. The fact remains; you will have a soul departure at some point. If you've never seen the bumper sticker, let me enlighten you. No God, No Peace. Know God, Know Peace.

Maybe you have read this book and thought; you guys make Jesus sound as though He is a real person. He is! Of all of the religions that have come and gone and of those still in existence, only one God, Jehovah, sent His only Son to die for your sins. God knew that you and I would never be "good enough," and so He sent his Son to take our place for our sins. Surely you are at least a little intrigued by a man whose life historically has more support of His existence than Julius Caesar! Not to mention, who predicts His own death and resurrection and then does it! I'm not sure about you, but if one of my buddies at work, or a neighbor told me, "Hey – I'm dying this Friday, but relax…I'll be back on Sunday," I'd think they'd lost their marbles!

That, however, is what Jesus said, and what Jesus did. If He really is not important, why does He remain such a pivotal part of our world as well as such a hot and debatable subject? How can such a non-issue be such an issue?

Now, I encourage you to ask the One who created you to reinstate your purpose and get after it. You have one life; what will you do with it? As for me, I'm going to use it all up encouraging others to use it all up for something that will last long after they're gone.

The whole greatness concept may be new to you. Truthfully, I'm still trying to wrap my head around it. You've had a great deal of opportunity to peek into my life through this book. Remember the first moment when the front cover caught your attention? Even if at this point, you've not yet changed a thing, I urge you now to take a good long look in the mirror to see what greatness looks like. See? It was there all the time.

An entry by Kathleen Palumbo

A story complete? Certainly not mine. On the topic of works in progress it was my wish to weigh in on the journey of penning this book. One cannot simply take part in the writing of a memoir such as David's and not be changed by it. Although it was quite some time ago that David shared his story/testimony with me, it was through the process of actually writing it that I in a sense relived the events of his life.

I met David in elementary school. The David of whom he speaks as a kindred spirit to Chris, the David with attention issues, the David who struggled. He and I would attend different high schools and our paths wouldn't cross again until more than 25 years later when he was scheduled to speak at Canfield High School, where I was at the time employed. To say I was mesmerized by the power he had over the students to whom he spoke would be an understatement. This was most certainly not the David I remembered. I would witness that command again as he spoke at the middle, elementary, and athletic levels over the next few years, and from time to time, the topic of collaborating on a book would come up. I know I'm not the only person who brought to his attention that his story was worth putting on paper, nor the only one to offer assisting in the endeavor, however, there arrived one fateful day when I received a text message from David stating simply, "I'm ready."

I am honored to have been entrusted with this piece of artwork, as that is what his story on paper is to me...artwork. Not the kind one can simply create on their own, but the kind driven by divine intervention. Do I think for one moment that our crossing paths at CHS that day was a coincidence? That having the opportunity to see him impacting students again and again was happenstance? That God wasn't steering that ship all along? Absolutely not! What do I believe? I believe that my passion for writing is God-given. I believe that He brings people into our lives and sometimes back into our lives for very good reasons. I believe that as someone who knew the *before* David, I was best able to see the transformation to the *after* David and to bring his story to all of you. I believe that I am beyond blessed to have been that person. As David stated, God doesn't make mistakes.

If you gain anything from reading David's story, it is my hope that you will carry his message around in your heart; that there is a purpose for your life. That as long as you walk this earth there is an unfinished story in your existence, and most importantly, that it is when you stop fooling yourself into believing that you are in control and turn the steering wheel of your life over to God that things begin to make sense.

I have found personally that a sense of peace is possible only where there is faith. Faith came full circle for me as so many in turn believed in my ability to bring this book to your hands, thus urging me along. To my mom, whom I lost during this book writing journey, my dad, who passed many years ago but not before encouraging my dreams; my husband Fred; my children; Nick and Emily; David Kohout himself; and many friends I've made along the way. My heart is full with gratitude.

I leave you with a favorite Bible verse of my own, one that interestingly enough found its way across my path numerous times during this book writing voyage. I hope that once you've closed this book and begun to think in terms of "greatness," that it brings you peace of mind along the way.

"Don't worry about anything; instead, pray about everything; tell God your needs and don't forget to thank Him for His answers. If you do this you will experience God's peace, which is far more wonderful than the human mind can understand. His peace will keep your thoughts and your hearts quiet as you trust in Christ Jesus."

ACKNOWLEDGEMENTS

To Victor, who in 1981 challenged me to pray, "God, if You are real, help me."

To Aunt Doris and Uncle Frank Dixon, thank you for loving me when I wasn't so lovable and for praying that God would get ahold of my heart and life. He sure did!

Mom, Dad, Aunt Marg, Lori, Barbara, and Jeff, thank you for praying and begging God to break through my selfishness, bitterness, and unforgiving and hurtful heart; He heard you.

To the young man who had the guts to walk into a laundromat in Kill Devil Hills, NC in August of that same year and attempt to share how Jesus Christ could help me if only I'd ask, not knowing that just three weeks earlier I had prayed just that! Because of your love for the Lord and the lost He called you to reach out. You'll never know until Glory that I finally did bow to Someone greater than myself and let Him take over.

Thank you to Fred and Liz Markusic, for allowing me to ask more questions than the rest of your entire group of folks at Sunday school and couple's studies. Your patience allowed my spirit to be taught, challenged, and matured into the man God has made me today.

Steve and Kathy Blakeman, who watched a 21 year old clueless salesman cold call your new office and a few months later, become a part of your team for the next 15 years…what a ride! What a great experience. I am in large part who I am today because of your mentorship, leadership, and encouragement.

My bride…May 4th, 1985 was just the beginning of the best part of my life. Your patience, your forgiveness, and your willingness to NEVER bring up something from the past, are incredible qualities I could never have survived without. Thank you for our beautiful children; the apples of our eyes! We have both been so blessed because of them.

Pastor Fred Mayhew, you had the wisdom and courage to release me to go meet other pastors and men who might be able to help connect and point me in the right direction. That wisdom was life changing.

Mike and Elaine; I could not have asked for a better second set of parents.

Bob Stauffer, you took a chance and hired me into the ministry of Fellowship of Christian Athletes when I had no clue what FCA even stood for. When you said "Take good and lay it at the altar of best," I had no idea what you were talking about. I do now!

To Kim and Jim Poma, your belief in me and your financial seed gift to Talk is Cheap was just the beginning of just how amazing God would be and has been. I am eternally grateful.

To Doc Sansone, your help and support helped make me who I am today.

Mike and Marney, when I opened your email on Thursday, January 12th, 2006, I could not believe what I read; but you did what you said you would do, and now more than 500,000 students all over the United States and in four other countries can in part thank you for sowing into me when we hadn't yet figured out what Talk is Cheap would be or do!

Dr./Pastor Brent Allen, thank you for helping me when I had already begun to lose hope in Talk is Cheap before we had even started.

To Karen Bovard and Judy Sees, who worked tirelessly until our tax exempt status was granted. I could never say thank you enough!

Tod and Al, I would not be Talk is Cheap without your wisdom and help.

Mr. Greg Smith, you saw a diamond when all I saw was coal! Thank you for your emotional, mental, and financial support; the investment you have made will only be known in its entirety in Glory.

To Bishop David Thomas, whom I had the honor of teaching and ministering alongside in Oslo, Norway, thank you for writing the "Teachers Gift," and encouraging me to believe there could be a book in me! You Sir, were correct!

To my Board of Directors, my Advisory Board, and the many faithful donors who said "Just go tell kids they matter." We have, I did, and I believe because of your support and encouragement, we will see the number of 500,000 plus students someday pale by comparison.

Thanks to Jim and Sue Rosa for your time, treasure, and talent. You make the best and coolest IRS cakes ever!

Dr. Chuck McGowen, my mentor for the past 10 years; much of who I have become is because of you. Thank you for your investment of time, wisdom, and the encouragement you poured into me. As Dave Zanotti once said, "You are a national treasure!" I love you and am honored to call you my brother, my mentor, and my friend. Eternity is going to be a blast with you and Jesus.

To my family…all of you! None of this happens without you. Period! Thank you. I love you.

Last but not least, by any stretch, Kathy Caputo Palumbo. Are you kidding me? We wrote a book!! Who knew when we attended St. Charles school together that one day God would allow us to cross paths again; this time with me speaking in the school building in which you worked. As Bob Stauffer used to say, "If you didn't know any better, you'd think God knew what he was doing!" Kathy, working with you on this gift of love has been a wonderful and encouraging experience. Your professionalism and expertise made this entire experience far less painful than I had always imagined. As this book sits in the hands of the reader, all I can say to you is thank you, God bless you, and welcome to the ride! Only God knows what happens now as the world reads my story and the amazing gift you have of capturing it and putting it into words. I am thankful for our friendship; I AM STANDING IN THE PRESENCE OF GREATNESS! SITPOG!

BIBLIOGRAPHY

Chapter 3. "Go the Distance." Jim Serger. Advantage Media
    Group. Oct. 2011.
Chapter 4. "Experiencing God." Dr. Henry Blackaby. Oct.
    1990
Chapter 4. "From Your Head to Your Heart." Maria Durso.
    Create Space Publishing. Feb. 2015

ABOUT THE AUTHOR

If you've read this book in its entirety, you've become familiar with David Kohout's goal in reaching out to our youth and his 28 years of experience in doing so, the last nine, through Talk is Cheap, Inc.

In seven brief chapters, David has shared with you just how the power of Greatness changed his life and in a sense, takes those experiences and others on the road to share his gift of speaking publicly, inspiring everyone who hears him to dig deep and find that seed of greatness within themselves.

Married for 31 years to his high school sweetheart, David and his wife Susie still reside in the Youngstown area where Talk is Cheap, Inc. got its start, and together, they now dedicate their lives to its purpose.

Please visit Talk is Cheap, Inc.'s website @ TalkisCheapinc. com for additional information. If you would like to arrange a speaking engagement, please contact either David Kohout, at david@talkischeapinc.com, or Susan Kohout, at susan@talkischeapinc.com.

If this book has moved you toward making some changes in your life, spread the word, share the book with another, arrange to have David speak at your church, place of employment, or local school, and pay that change forward. It is through movement like this that eventually virtually everyone will realize that they are in fact standing in the presence of greatness.

ABOUT THE AUTHOR

Taking a step back from numerous years of writing experience for four divisions of the Town Crier Community Newspapers wherein she authored primarily human interest stories, Kathleen Palumbo approached her first book writing endeavor with Standing in the Presence of Greatness, calling it a labor of love and a journey reconnecting her with her own faith.

Finding a certain synchronicity between sharing the stories of her newspaper subjects and collaborating on Standing in the Presence of Greatness to bring David's story to the hands of all of you, it is with this project that Kathleen felt the magnitude of possibility that the message carried within could resonate around the world.

Operating on the belief that it is only in recognizing ourselves as difference-making beings, we often need to make a change within ourselves before we can make a difference in the world whether we seek to transform our own personal world, our own little corner of it, or far reaching change.

If you would like to offer feedback on how Standing in the Presence of Greatness' message has inspired or encouraged you to see the greatness in yourself, or if you have a story of your own you'd like help in sharing, Kathleen Palumbo can be contacted via email at kpalumbo6@gmail.com.

A free eBook edition is available with the purchase of this book.

To claim your free eBook edition:

1. Download the Shelfie app.
2. Write your name in upper case in the box.
3. Use the Shelfie app to submit a photo.
4. Download your eBook to any device.

Shelfie

A free eBook edition is available
with the purchase of this print book.

CLEARLY PRINT YOUR NAME ABOVE IN UPPER CASE

Instructions to claim your free eBook edition:
1. Download the Shelfie app for Android or iOS
2. Write your name in **UPPER CASE** above
3. Use the Shelfie app to submit a photo
4. Download your eBook to any device

Print & Digital Together Forever.

Snap a photo

Free eBook

Read anywhere

CPSIA information can be obtained
at www.ICGtesting.com
Printed in the USA
LVOW03s1258210318
570641LV00001B/1/P